Let's Visit the Fire Station

Marianne Johnston

The Rosen Publishing Group's
PowerKids Press ™
New York

Published in 2000 by The Rosen Publishing Group, Inc.
29 East 21st Street, New York, NY 10010

First Edition

Book Design: Danielle Primiceri

Photo Credits:Cover © 1979 Gary Benson; p. 4 © Blair Seitz/Photo Researchers, Inc.; p. 7 © CORBIS/Bettmann; p. 8 © Richard Hutchings/Photo Researchers, Inc., SuperStock; p. 11 © GRANTPIX/Photo Researchers, Inc., Superstock; p. 12 © Superstock; p. 15 © Linda Phillips/Photo Researchers, Inc.; p. 16 © 1992 Susan Kuklin/Photo Researchers, Inc.; p. 17 © Joseph Nettis/Photo Researchers, Inc.; p. 19 © Scott Barrow/International Stock; p. 20 © Charlie Westerman/International Stock.

Johnston, Marianne.
        Let's's visit the fire station / by Marianne Johnston.
                p.   cm. — (Our community)
        Includes index.
        Summary: Describes fire stations, the functions they perform, and the role they play
in the community.
        ISBN 0-8239-5435-8 (lib. bdg. : alk. paper)
        1. Fire extinction—Juvenile literature. 2. Fire stations—Juvenile literature. [1. Fire extinction. 2. Fire stations.] I. Title. II. Series: Johnston, Marianne. Our community.
TH9148.J67   1999
363.37—dc21   99-19176
                                                                                    CIP

Manufactured in the United States of America

CONTENTS

Fire Stations Are 'Help' Stations

When you hear a siren, does your heart race a bit faster? Hearing those big red trucks as they hurry to put out fires, and often to save lives, is exciting.

Those firefighters and their trucks come from a fire station in the **community**. The fire station is where fire trucks and firefighters stay when there are no emergencies. A fire station is also a place that you can go to for help. Firefighters are always happy to help you if you are hurt or in trouble.

◀ *It can be exciting to see fire trucks leaving the station.*

The History of Firefighting

Around 300 years ago, there were no fire stations in our country. When a fire broke out, the community formed a **bucket brigade**, lining up and passing buckets of water to put out the fire. People started using water pumps to fight fires about 200 years ago. Pumps worked better than buckets of water because they could get more water onto a fire in less time. Fire stations were created to provide a place to store the pumps.

6

Water pumps made it easier for people to put out fires. ▶

Today's Fire Stations

Fire stations, which are sometimes called fire houses, usually have two floors. The bottom floor is where the fire trucks are parked. The fire captain's office and the front desk are downstairs, too. The top floor is where the firefighters stay when they are not busy. Most firefighters work 24 hours at a time. They eat and sleep at the station. The firefighters must also clean the fire station.

FUN FACTS

When there is a fire, the firefighters slide down a long, steel pole from the top floor to the bottom.

The station house is a second home to most firefighters.

The Fire Call

When someone needs the fire department to come and put out a fire, she calls the emergency number for her community. The emergency operator contacts the fire department **dispatcher**. The dispatcher's job is to figure out which fire station is closest to the site of the fire. Then the dispatcher sends a message, either by computer or by using the fire station bells, to that fire station. Alarms go off at the community fire station.

Sometimes the fire station has a computer that prints out the location of the fire. ▶

The Engine Company

When they're fighting fires, firefighters split up into groups called companies. One group is called the engine company. They are in charge of the truck with the hoses, called a fire engine. The **engineer** drives the fire engine and hooks the engine up to a nearby fire **hydrant**. The rest of the engine company grab the hoses off the back of the truck and head for the fire. Water flows from the hydrant and shoots out of the hoses.

FUN FACTS

Fire engines have a tank inside them that holds 500 gallons of water.

◀ *The engine pump pushes water from the hydrant out of the hoses.*

The Truck Company

Another group of firefighters is the truck company. These firefighters operate the fire truck without the hoses. This truck has an **aerial ladder** sitting on top of it. Once they get to the fire, members of the truck company punch holes in the roof, windows, or walls of the burning building. This lets the smoke out. Next, they enter the building and search for people who need help getting out.

FUN FACTS

The aerial ladder can extend to 100 feet. It is used to reach people who are trapped in tall buildings and can't get out.

14

This fire truck also has lots of smaller ladders and other equipment. ▶

Firefighters' Gear

Before they fight a fire, firefighters have to put on about 50 pounds of **equipment**. The **fireproof** pants that firefighters wear are already attached to their boots. After they get into these pants, they put their fireproof coats on. They also wear oxygen tanks on their backs to help them breathe inside a burning building. Helmets made of leather or plastic protect firefighters' heads from falling pieces of the building.

◄ *Firefighters have lots of equipment to help them fight fires.*

FUN FACTS

The "hook" is a thin pole with a metal hook on the end of it. Firefighters use it to rescue people.

17

First Aid

When people are pulled from a fire, they often need medical help right away. Firefighters must know a lot about **first aid** to help an injured person. They sometimes have to keep the victims alive until an ambulance or doctor can get there. Firefighters also help people who are hurt in car accidents. They do this because they know a lot about first aid, and because a car that has been in an accident often catches on fire.

18

Our communities depend on these men and women for more than fighting fires.

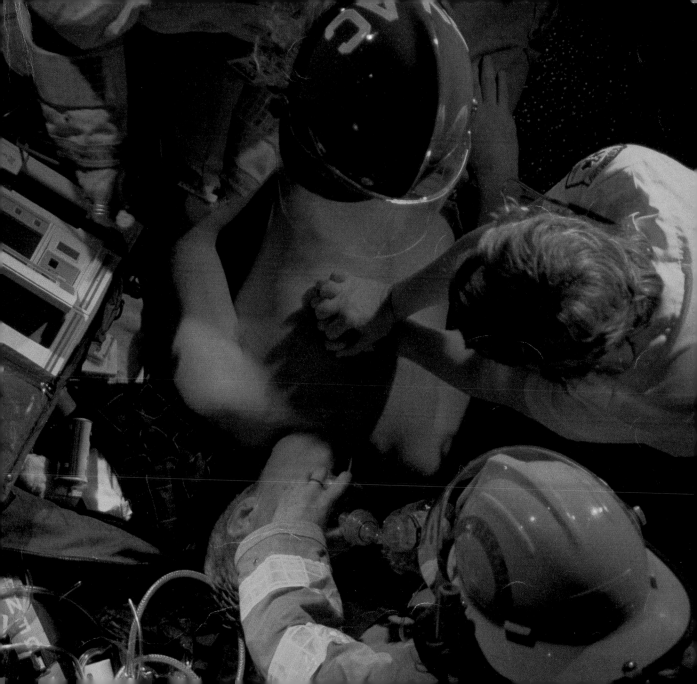

Technology in Firefighting

Technology has helped firefighters do their jobs better. Before computers existed, most dispatchers used bells in the fire station to ring out a code, telling the firefighters which street or block the fire was on.

Today, all firefighters wear beepers strapped to their oxygen tanks. If the firefighter doesn't move for more than 20 seconds, the beeper sends out a very loud beep with a flashing light. This way other firefighters can find him if he is hurt.

In the past, if a firefighter was hurt, the others would have no way to find him.

Fire Prevention

The best way to fight fires is through **fire prevention**. Teaching the community how to stop a fire before it starts is a big part of a firefighter's job. When they are not out battling fires, firefighters are responsible for making sure people follow all fire safety laws.

Web Sites:

For more information on fire stations, check out these Web sites:

http://www.hvfd.com

http://camalott.com/abilene/firedept

GLOSSARY

aerial ladder (AYR-ee-ul LA-dur) The ladder that lies along the top of the fire truck and is used for reaching people in tall buildings.

bucket brigade (BUH-keht brih-GAYD) The line people used to form to fight fires by using buckets of water.

community (kum-MYOO-nih-tee) A group of people who have something in common, such as a special interest or the area where they live.

dispatcher (DIS-pach-er) The person at the central fire department who routes emergency calls to the local fire stations.

engineer (ehn-jin-EER) The firefighter who drives the engine truck to the scene of the fire.

equipment (ee-KWIP-mint) The supplies needed to carry out an activity.

fire prevention (FY-ur pruh-VEHN-shun) Doing things to make sure a fire doesn't start in the first place.

fireproof (FY-ur PROOF) When something cannot catch on fire.

first aid (FURST AYD) Emergency treatment for an injury before the person can get to the hospital.

hydrant (HY-drint) The short, steel pipe near the curb that fire engines use to get water.

technology (tek-NAH-loh-gee) Using science to solve problems.

23

INDEX